Gisela is going home to Rio de Janeiro after a month's vacation in London. She lives in an apartment in Rio with two friends.

Her airplane leaves at five o'clock. It is one o'clock now.

Gisela puts her clothes and a manuscript into a travel bag. This manuscript is very important to her. She is writing her first book.

1

Ricardo is a student. He lives in Rio de Janeiro. After two months in England, he is going home.

He finds his seat on the airplane. A pretty girl is sitting in the seat near him.

"Hi!" Ricardo says to the girl. He smiles at her.

Gisela looks up, but she doesn't smile.

"Hello," she says, and she looks down at her book again.

Suddenly, Ricardo's bag falls on the girl. It knocks the book from her hands.

"Oh!" Gisela says.

"Sorry!" Ricardo says. "I'm sorry!" He quickly gets her book from the floor and looks at it. "Interesting," he says. "Here you are."

"Thank you," she says. She is annoyed.

"My name's Ricardo," Ricardo says.

Gisela looks up at him.

"Is it?" she says. Then she looks at her book again.

"What's your name?" he asks.

Gisela doesn't look up from her book this time.

"Gisela," she says.

"That's a pretty name," Ricardo says.

Ricardo is talking about his time in England.

"I like London," he says. "I like the noise, the lights, the people, the red buses. Do you like London, Gisela? Do you like England?"

Gisela puts down her book and sighs.

"Yes," she says. "I like London. I like England. And I like *quiet* people!"

Later, there is a movie. Ricardo is watching the movie, but after a time he sleeps. Very slowly, his head falls onto Gisela's shoulder.

Gisela looks at Ricardo and sighs.

"I don't *want* his head on my shoulder," she thinks. "But he is *quiet* now." She thinks about her manuscript. "I can finish the story in Rio," she thinks.

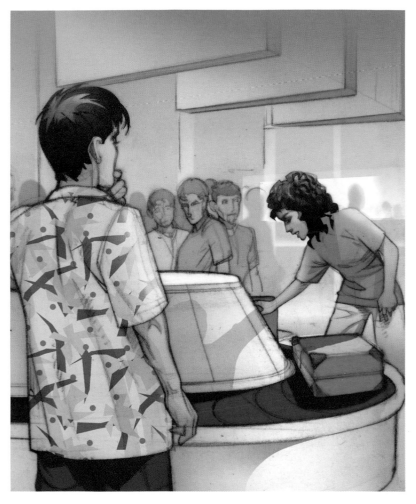

Many hours later, the airplane arrives at Rio de Janeiro airport. Gisela and Ricardo go into the building and wait for their bags.

Gisela's bag is blue. Suddenly, she sees a blue travel bag. "Here it is!" she thinks. "Good. Now I can go—and Ricardo can't follow me."

She quickly takes the bag and leaves the airport.

Ricardo watches Gisela.

"Wait for me, Gisela!" he thinks. But he doesn't have his bag. He can't leave the airport.

Then, suddenly, he sees a blue travel bag.

"That's my bag!" he thinks. "Maybe I can catch Gisela!"

He quickly takes the blue bag and runs from the airport into the street.

And there is Gisela, on a bus!

"Wait!" Ricardo calls.

He runs after the bus, but the bus doesn't stop for him.

Gisela sees Ricardo from the window of the bus, and
she smiles.

But now Ricardo is looking down at the blue bag.

"Something's wrong," he thinks.

The bus is very hot and Gisela's eyes close. She sleeps after the long journey from London.

A man on the bus is looking at the blue travel bag.

"Maybe there's money in that bag, or some expensive clothes," he thinks.

The bus is stopping now. Quickly, the man takes the bag and runs.

The bus stops and Gisela opens her eyes. Then the bus moves again and she sees the man. He is running down the street with the blue bag.

"Stop! Stop the bus!" Gisela says. "That man has my bag!"

The bus stops again and Gisela runs after the man. But where is he?

Gisela runs up and down the streets of Rio, but she can't see the thief. She is angry and unhappy.

"My manuscript!" she thinks. "It's in that bag! Months and months of work! What can I do now? I can't start again."

Then, slowly, Gisela walks home to her apartment building.

Ricardo is waiting for her at the door!

"What do *you* want, Ricardo?" Gisela says. "Oh! Is that my bag?"

Ricardo smiles. "*I* have your bag and *you* have—" He stops. "Where is it? Where's my bag?"

"*Your* bag?" Gisela says. "Oh! I'm sorry. A thief has your bag!"

The thief is looking at the things in Ricardo's bag. He doesn't understand. They aren't the clothes of a pretty young woman.

"What's this?" he thinks. "Dirty shirts! Dirty old jeans!"

He looks for some money or an expensive dress, but he doesn't find them.

He leaves the clothes in the street and walks away.

"I have my manuscript!" Gisela says. *"Thank* you."

Ricardo laughs. "And the thief can have my old shirts
and jeans!" he says. "A big mistake!"

She smiles at him. "A lucky mistake for me," she says.
"But how—?"

"How do I know your address?" Ricardo says. "It's on
the label. You read books, Gisela. I read *labels*!"

# ACTIVITIES

*Before you read*

1 Look at the Word List at the back of the book. What are the words in your language?

2 Read about the story on the back of the book.

    **a**  Where are Ricardo and Gisela going?

    **b**  What does Gisela like?

    **c**  What does Ricardo like?

    **d**  Who takes Gisela's bag?

3 Look at the picture on page 2. What is the right answer?

    **a**  Gisela and Ricardo are *young / old*.

    **b**  They go on *a train / an airplane*.

    **c**  It is *hot / cold* there.

*While you read*

4 Are the sentences right (✓) or wrong (✗)?

    **a**  Gisela lives in London.    .....

    **b**  She is writing a book.    .....

    **c**  Ricardo lives in Rio.    .....

    **d**  He sits near Gisela on the airplane.    .....

    **e**  Gisela watches a movie and then sleeps.    .....

    **f**  Gisela has a green bag.    .....

5 Answer the questions. Write sentences.

    **a**  What color is Ricardo's bag?

    ..........................................................................................

    **b**  Does Gisela wait for Ricardo at the airport?

    ..........................................................................................

**c** How does she go into Rio from the airport?

.........................................................................................................

**d** Why does she run after a man?

.........................................................................................................

**e** Where is Ricardo waiting for Gisela?

.........................................................................................................

**f** Who has Gisela's bag?

.........................................................................................................

**g** Who has Ricardo's bag?

.........................................................................................................

**h** What is on Gisela's bag?

.........................................................................................................

*After you read*

**6** The thief makes a big mistake, but it is a lucky mistake for Gisela. Talk with a friend about one of your big mistakes. Do you laugh about it now, or not?

**7** Work with a friend.

*Student A*:  You are Gisela. Talk about Ricardo and the big mistake.

*Student B*:  You are Gisela's friend. Ask questions.

**8** Ricardo and Gisela like London. What town do you like? Why? Write about it.

**9** Gisela is writing her first book. It is a story: "A Winter Morning." How does it start? Write three or four sentences.

## WORD LIST *with example sentences*

**annoyed** (adj) I am not angry, but I am *annoyed.*

**clothes** (n pl) They are buying new *clothes.* The children don't have coats for the winter.

**dirty** (adj) Please wash your *dirty* hands!

**follow** (v) We are going in our car. You can *follow* us in your car.

**hour** (n) It is an *hour* on the bus from my home to my office.

**journey** (n) Take the car. The *journey* is very long on the train.

**knock** (v) He often *knocks* things onto the floor.

**label** (n) This is my bag. My name and address are on the *label.*

**laugh** (v) Why are you *laughing?* I like this hat.

**leave** (v) I am *leaving* work now and I am going home.

**lucky** (adj) They live in that beautiful house. They are very *lucky.*

**manuscript** (n) This is the *manuscript* of my father's new book.

**mistake** (n) Oh, do I have your coat? Sorry about the *mistake.*

**pretty** (adj) She is a *pretty* child, but not very smart.

**seat** (n) Excuse me! 20C is my *seat.*

**shoulder** (n) The boy can't see the game. Put him on your *shoulders.*

**sigh** (v) Are you *sighing?* The job is not difficult!

**something** (pron) There is *something* on the floor. What is it?

**travel** (n) She likes *travel* and she visits interesting places.

**thief** (n) *Thieves* are taking bags from trains at night.

**Pearson Education Limited**
Edinburgh Gate, Harlow,
Essex CM20 2JE, England
and Associated Companies throughout the world.

ISBN: 978-1-4058-7670-4

First published 2002
This edition first published 2008

3 5 7 9 10 8 6 4 2

Typeset by Graphicraft Ltd, Hong Kong
Set in 12/20pt Life Roman
Printed in China
SWTC/02

Published by Pearson Education Ltd in association with
Penguin Books Ltd, both companies being subsidiaries of Pearson Plc

For a complete list of the titles available in the Penguin Readers series please write
to your local Pearson Longman office or to: Penguin Readers Marketing Department,
Pearson Education, Edinburgh Gate, Harlow, Essex CM20 2JE, England.